Bernard the Blue Lobster

Michael King

Copyright © 2024 by Michael King

ISBN: 978-1-960764-65-2(sc)
ISBN: 978-1-960764-66-9 (hc)

All rights reserved. No part of this publication may be reproduced, distributed, or transmitted in any form or by any means, including photocopying, recording, or other electronic or mechanical methods, without the prior written permission of the author, except in the case of brief quotations embodied in critical reviews and certain other non-commercial uses permitted by copyright law.

Write and Release
PUBLISHING

www.writeandreleasepublishing.com

For Mom and Dad, who taught me that in a world full of Sallys, it's always best to be a Bernard.

It was a gloomy sort of day in Sea Shanty Bay and Bernard was feeling down. He was a little concerned about the weather, but it was then he heard the voice of his friend.

"Bernard, let's go to the Kelp Beds," called Carla Crab.

"I don't know," said Bernard as he came out from under the wharf, "I think there is bad weather coming. I might stay home."

"Alright, let's go!" said Bernard.

The two were having lots of fun playing when suddenly they heard a voice say angrily, "What are you doing? You can't play here!"

The voice belonged to Sally, a prickly sea urchin who never liked Bernard. She thought lobsters should be red, not blue!

"I never gave you permission to play here," Sally snapped. "Especially you, Bluey, with your big ugly claw. Get Lost Weirdo!"

Suddenly Max the Mussel turned to Sally and said, "You don't own the Kelp Beds.

Anyone can play here for as long as we like." But Bernard just sighed and said, "Let's go, we can play somewhere else."

The current seemed stronger as Bernard scuttled back to the wharf.

"Bernard, slow down, I can't keep up," said Carla trying not to get swept away.

"You shouldn't let Sally boss you around like that. We didn't have to leave."

Bernard looked at Carla with a smile and said, "You're right. We can have just as much fun playing here."

Bernard, Carla, and Max were enjoying their time together when Bernard stopped playing and took a look around.

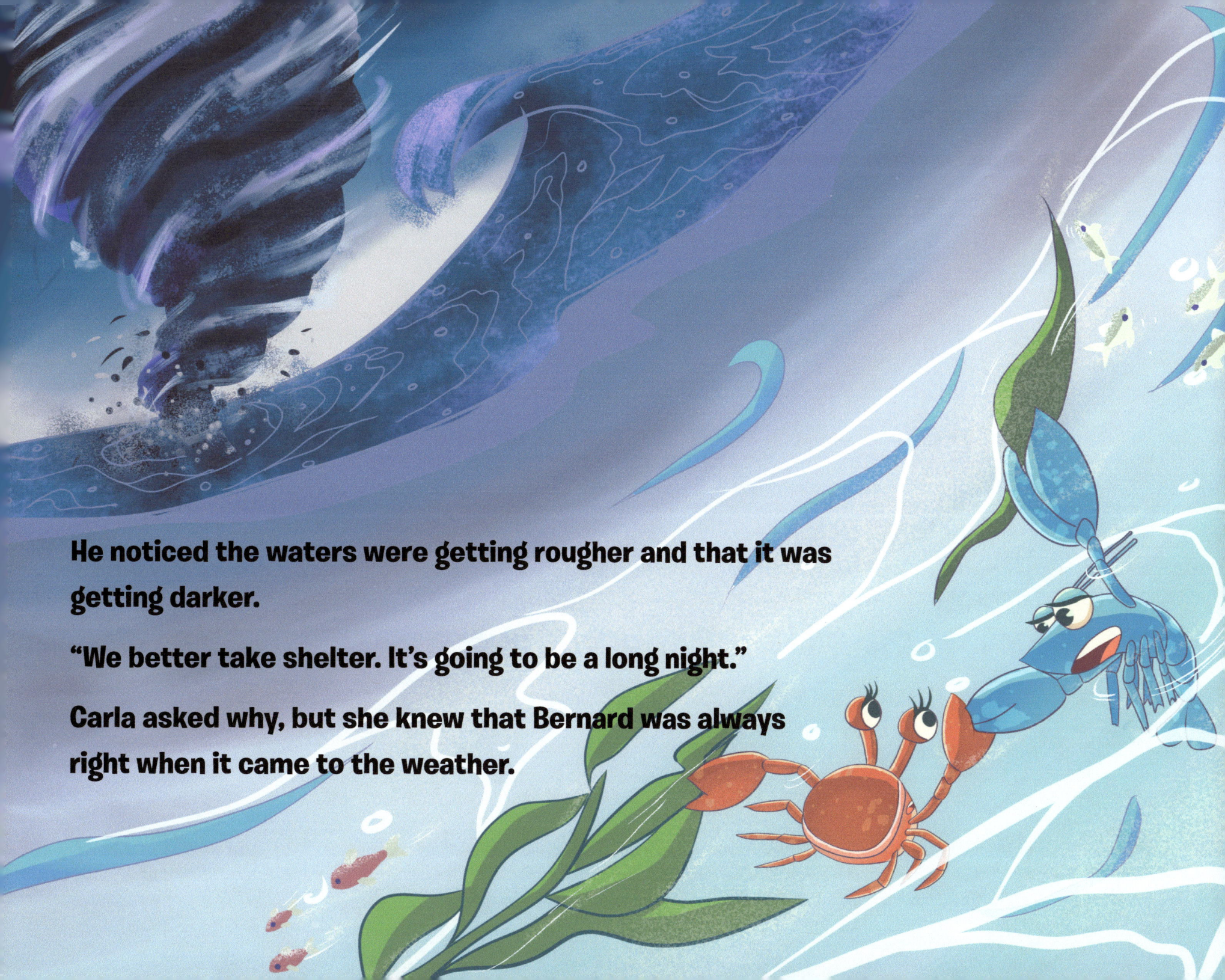

He noticed the waters were getting rougher and that it was getting darker.

"We better take shelter. It's going to be a long night."

Carla asked why, but she knew that Bernard was always right when it came to the weather.

Bernard looked at Carla and said, "I'm going to the Kelp Beds to warn everyone that there is a storm coming."

Bernard had to fight the current as he hurried back to the Kelp Beds. The water was murky and the kelp was swirling around making it hard to see. When he got there he saw that most of the other fish had already left.

Struggling against the current, Bernard yelled, "Hey everyone, There is a bad storm coming! You should all find somewhere to hide until the storm is over."

Sally quickly turned and said, "Don't listen to him! He's just a lobster, a blue lobster! He is not red like the other lobsters. What does he know about anything? Go away Bernard, no one wants you here."

Bernard, Carla, and Max spent the night under the wharf away from the storm. The following day Carla said, "Let's go see how much damage the storm caused."

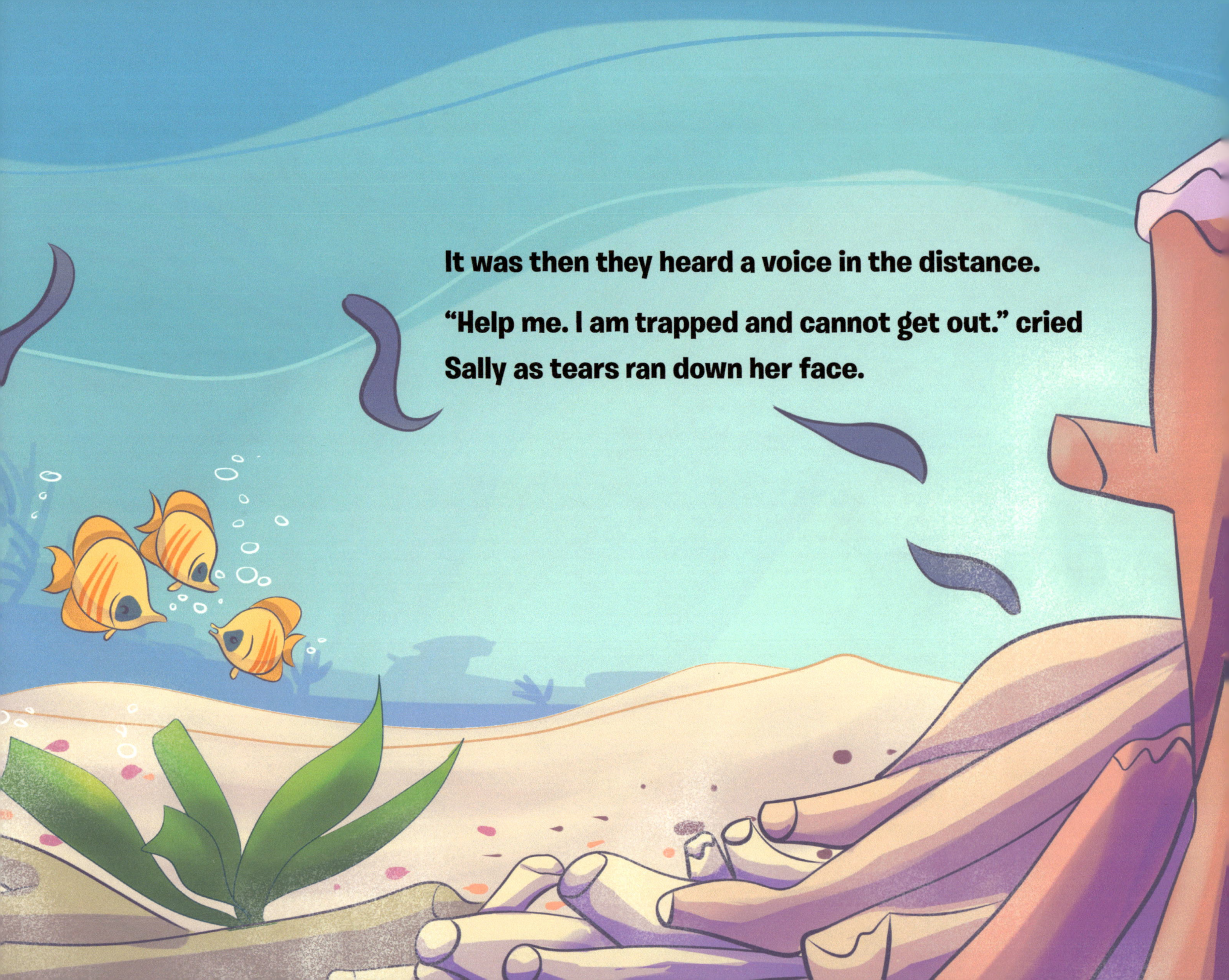

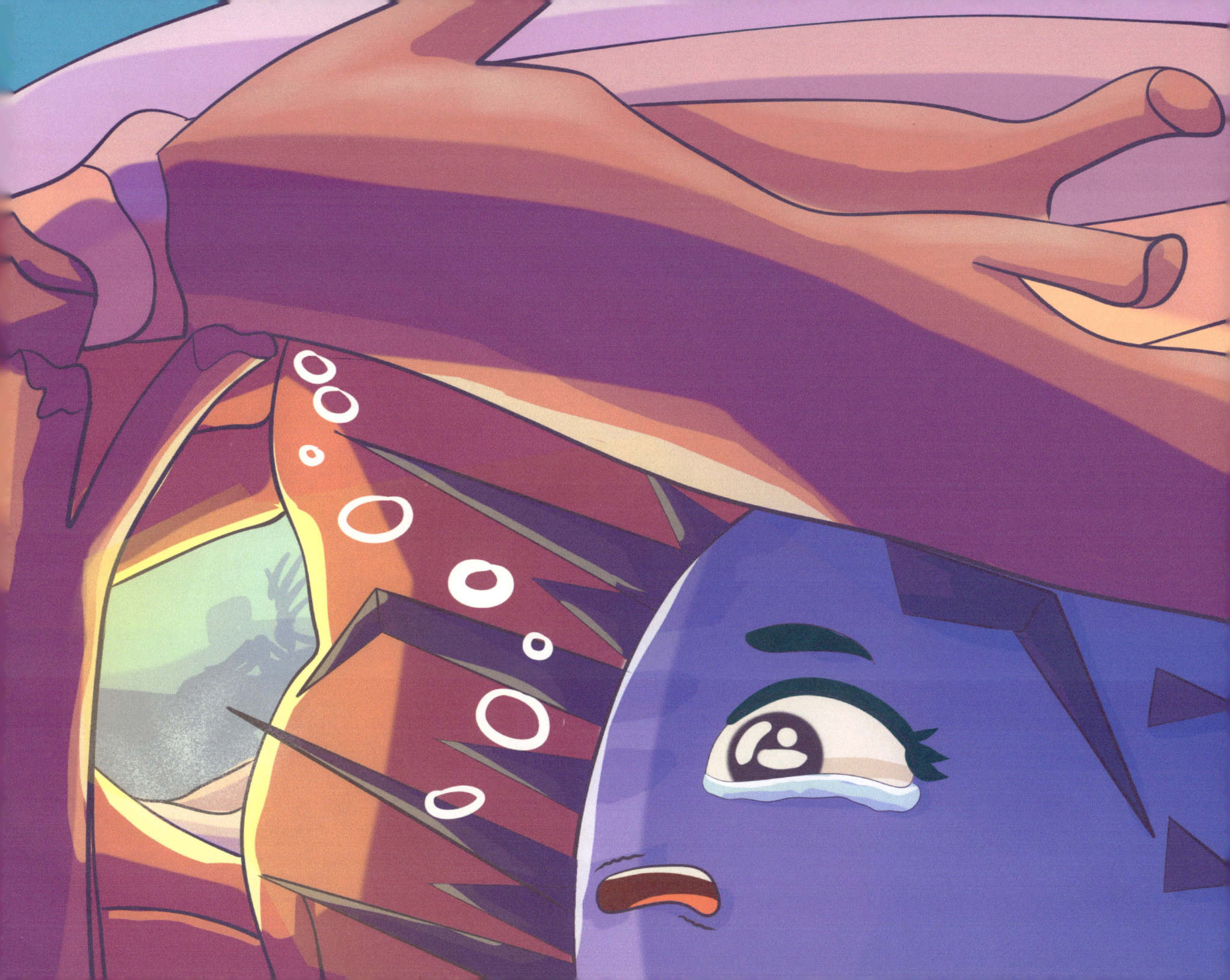

Bernard, Carla, and Max headed toward the voice and saw a small school of fish fluttering about. There was a pile of debris that they were trying to move but it was too heavy.

Bernard heard the whispers behind him saying "Don't help her. She has always been so mean. Just leave her there. She deserves it for not listening."

Carla looked at Bernard and asked, "What do you want to do? She always made fun of you because you are a blue lobster and have one big claw."

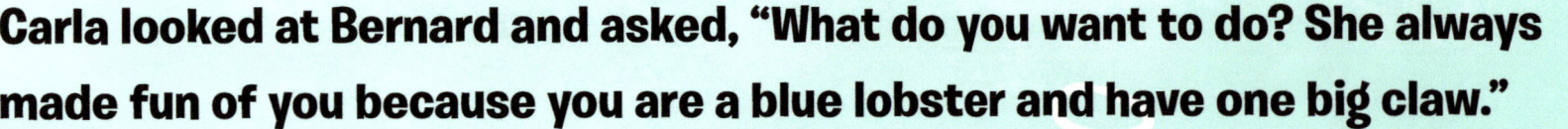

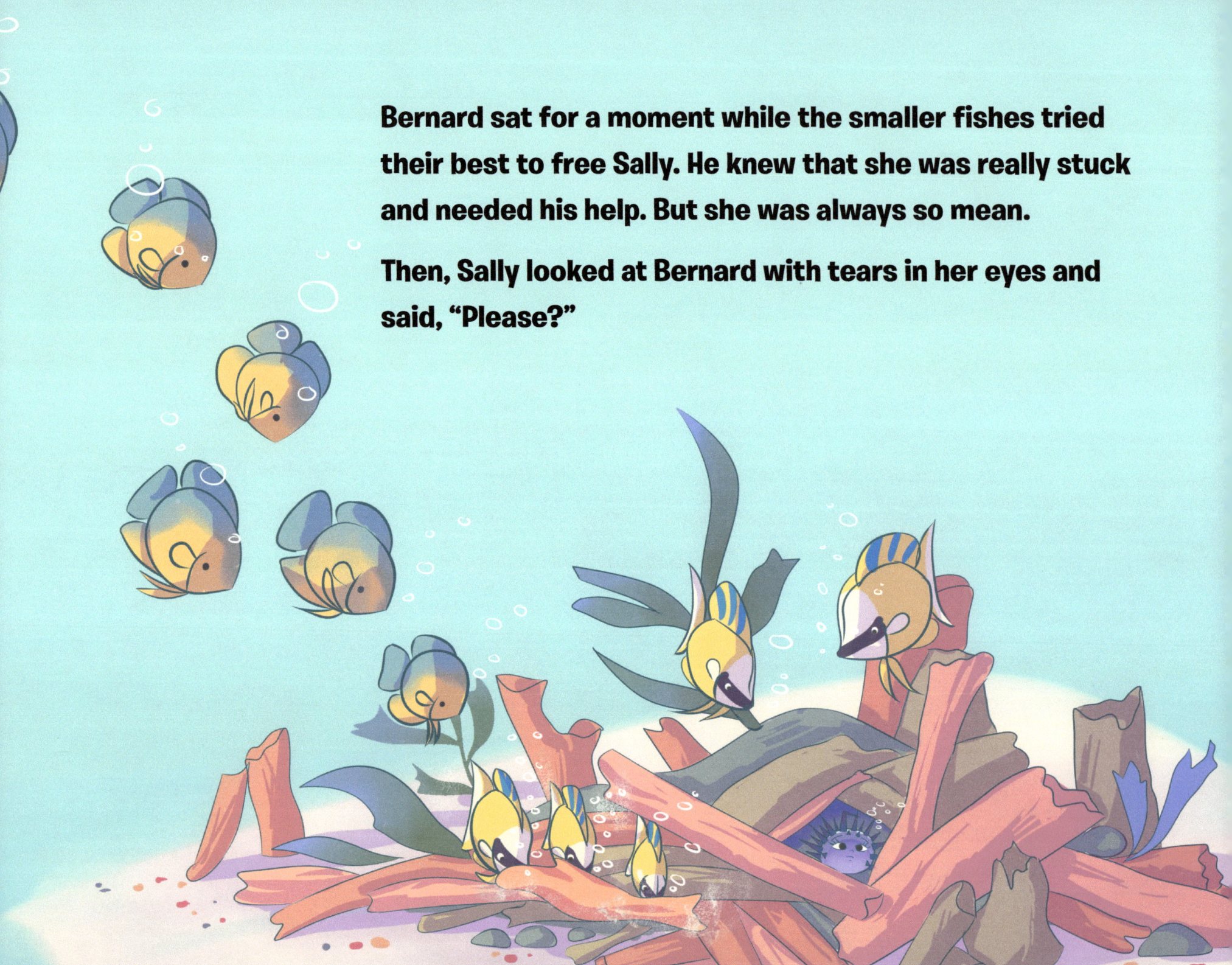

Bernard sat for a moment while the smaller fishes tried their best to free Sally. He knew that she was really stuck and needed his help. But she was always so mean.

Then, Sally looked at Bernard with tears in her eyes and said, "Please?"

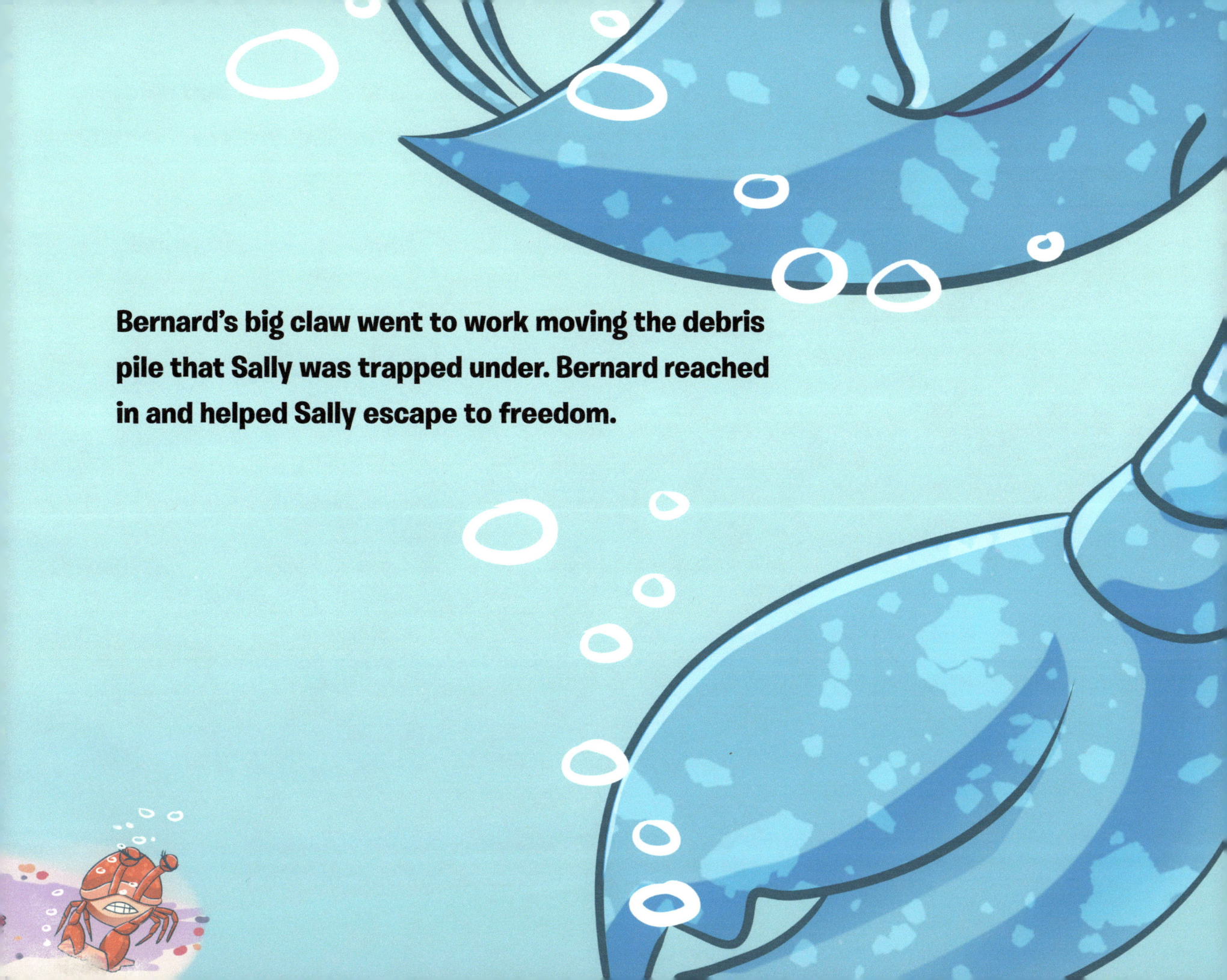

Bernard's big claw went to work moving the debris pile that Sally was trapped under. Bernard reached in and helped Sally escape to freedom.

Sally looked at Bernard with her head hung low and said, "I'm so sorry for being so mean to you. Can you forgive me? I will try to be a nicer person."

"It's okay Sally, I know you didn't mean it," said Bernard

Bernard and his friends went to the Kelp Beds to help clean up with Sally leading the way.

"You know what Bernard? Just because you are a blue lobster doesn't mean you are any different from the rest of us. I hope we can be friends." she reached out to him and gently held onto his claw.

www.ingramcontent.com/pod-product-compliance
Lightning Source LLC
Chambersburg PA
CBHW050848010526
44107CB00017BA/1216